Illustrated Circular Kent Walks

Illustrated Circular Kent Walks

BRIAN COLEMAN

CONTENTS

FOREWORD

During the Covid pandemic when we were all locked down, my wife and I started looking for walks in and around our home town. Although we had lived there for nearly thirty years, our busy lives had not allowed the luxury of so much free time and so we found walks and places that we never knew existed – all within a few miles of home.

Soon we had exhausted all the local footpaths and byways and so I invested in many Ordnance Survey maps of Kent and started looking for circular walks of around 4-5 miles that we could do on Sundays and high days. Some worked, some didn't. The ones that worked can be found in this book. Over the years we have purchased several books of circular walks in Kent and some of the directions have not been accurate, leaving us to abandon the walks on occasion. With that in mind, I have tried to give as much information as possible in my directions, including pictures of strategic junction points. As a bonus, many start and finish at pubs!

Please note that some of the pictures showing paths crossing fields may change as the seasons progress and crops are grown or are harvested.

Enjoy!

Appledore

(6.5 miles)

Circular walk from the Ferry Inn, Stone-in-Oxney

The Ferry Inn is situated on the Appledore Road at Stone-in-Oxney. It's a 17th century pub with lots of character and a massive car park on the opposite of the road. They served fresh local fish as well as delicious home cooked food. It got its name as there used to be a ferry there when Oxney was an island. The English coast went all the way to Tenterden until all the land was reclaimed. Ferry Inn Postcode: TN30 7JY Tel: 01233 758246.

With your back to the pub, turn right and walk over the bridge, where there is a kiss gate on the right (picture 1) Walk along the Reading sewer as it winds along beside two fields, until you come to a footbridge and a kiss gate (picture 2) that leads you up a footpath over a large mound. As you reach a quiet road, look for the stile in the corner of the field. It's not very obvious until you are right on top of it (picture 3). Turn right and walk along the road until you come to the junction, with the church straight ahead.

| 1 | 2 | 3 – looking back after crossing |

Cross the road and turn right along the narrow pavement until you reach a foot-path to the left of the bridge. Go through and follow the Royal Military Canal, first past some new houses on the left (picture 4) and then for almost another 2 miles. There are some sheep grazing along this walk that are friendly. The canal was built during the Napoleonic wars as a defence. Further along you will see an old Second World war pill box set into the bank (picture 5). Carry on through another gate and finally you will come to a kiss gate just after a house on the left, which leads to a lane (picture 6).

| 4 | 5 | 6 |

Turn left and after a couple of yards, turn right onto a footpath across a field (picture 7). Be very careful on this path as the farmer has inconsiderately left a pile of manure on the path route. It looks solid, but as I found when I trod on it, looks can be deceiving and my leg plunged almost up to the knee in foul smelling silage! Carry on through a gap in the hedge (picture 8) and across a field heading for St. Mary's church at Kenardington (picture 9).

7   8   9

If you don't want to visit this church (which dates back to at least the 10th century), turn left at the gate before entering the graveyard and follow the path around the edge of the field to a gate in the corner (picture 10). Turn left and almost immediately on the right is a rather concealed gate into a field (picture 11) – blink and you'll miss it!

10   11

Carry on through two more gates and a small bridge over a stream (pictures 12 & 13) until you come to a vineyard. Carry on through the vineyards, past a line of trees to your right until you reach a post showing two footpath directions. Behind it is a beacon (picture 14). Turn left at this post and follow it under some power lines and past another vineyard. Go through a gate and keep going as straight as possible until you reach a small road with a house to the right and a playing field to the left.

12   13   14

Turn left onto the street and walk down to the church mentioned in the first chapter. Turn right and re-trace your steps back to the Ferry Inn.

Biggin Hill

(6 miles)

This walk is mainly a walk around the perimeter of the airfield, through fields, woodlands, lanes and the main road at the end. At certain points, we saw not only light aircraft take off, but also Lear jets, passenger jets and for a rare treat, a Spitfire, of which there are several in the Heritage hangar. They also offer flights to the paying public.

The walk starts when you park in Milking Lane in Leaves Green, either in the lane or the carpark of the Kings Arms, (postcode: BR2 6DU) now a Turkish restaurant (picture 1).

With your back to the pub, walk down the lane (picture 2) to the end and walk through the gap in the hedge (picture 3).

1   2   3

You will emerge onto a field of crops. Turn left and follow the footpath (picture 4). We visited in April, but the view will obviously be different in summer when the crops are higher. As you pass the back gardens of houses on you left, you will eventually meet a concreted lane (picture 5). Turn right and walk until you reach the trees and the 4-way footpath signpost (picture 6).

4   5   6

You need to take the path indicated by the rear left-hand sign that leads to a narrow path (picture 7). Carry on around the perimeter fence, past the gates and sign (pictures 8 & 9).

7   8   9

You will come to dilapidated large kiss gate (picture 10). Walk around the gate and continue on, over a large stile (picture 11) and eventually you will emerge onto Jail Lane (picture 12).

10   11   12

Turn left on Jail Lane, cross the road and walk along Old Tye Avenue (picture 13) and after a few paces, you will see a footpath on the right, next to a letter box (picture 14). Walk up this path, ignoring the fork to the left (picture 15). This area was regularly frequented by Charles Darwin, studying the flora and fauna when he lived in nearby village of Downe, at Downe House.

13   14   15

When you emerge onto the busy main road (picture 16), carefully cross the road and turn right. Walk until you see the Black Horse pub on the opposite side of the road and turn left down Hillcrest Road (picture 17). After passing a couple of houses on the right, walk down the footpath (picture 18).

16 17 18

The path ends at a cul de sac, with a very steep stepped path opposite (picture 19). Take this route and turn right when you reach a junction (picture 20). Carry on through the woodland until you reach some more steep steps to the left (picture 21).

19 20 21

When you reach a path between two houses (picture 22), turn right and after a few paces, look out for a sign post on the left (picture 23). Go down this path; turn right at the bottom and walk to the end of the street, where you will see a footpath sign high on a lamp post opposite (picture 24).

22   23   24

Walk up the road as it bends to the left, until you see another foot path sign on the right (picture 25). Follow this steep path, ignoring another path to the left, until it joins a dirt track (picture 26). Walk up this track to the junction of the main road and Salt Box hill (picture 27). Turn left on to the main road and walk along, past the Spitfire and Hurricane (main picture) until you are back to the start. Carefully cross the road.

25   26   27

Charing

(3.5 miles)

This walk starts at the Church of St. Peter and St. Paul, the parish church of Charing. It is situated next to the remains of the archbishop's palace, just off the high street. The church's west tower was built in the 14th century, though most of the rest of the building was reconstructed following a catastrophic fire in the 16th century. Parking can be difficult here, so you may have to park in School Road on the opposite side of the high street.

Walk back down school road to the roundabout and the fire station on your right (pictures 1 & 2).

Carefully cross the busy road and turn right, walking up the path until you come to a footpath sign on your left (picture 3).

1 2 3

Follow the path up across the field and across the horse racing course, to the hedge (pictures 4 & 5), when you will be on a byway. Ignore the footpath on the opposite side of the byeway (picture 6), but turn right and follow the byway.

4 5 6

When you reach a house ahead (picture 7) with an impressive clock house to you left, turn right and walk until you meet a main road. Turn left along this fast road and after a short while, carefully cross the road and continue down the byway marked "Pilgrims Way" (picture 8). After a while, ignore the fork to the right (picture 9), but carry straight on…

7   8   9

… until you reach a wooden seat with a footpath just before it on the right (picture 10). Follow this footpath until it reaches a lane and turn right (picture 11). After you pass some magnificent houses on the right, turn left along a path between two fields (picture 12).

10   11   12

Walk to another gate (picture 13) and across the field to some playing fields (pictures 14 & 15).

13   14   15

Continue until you come to a footpath on the right (picture 16). Walk down this path and after, turn right and this leads back through the church graveyard to the beginning.

16

Chilham

(4.5 miles)

Although this walk starts at the square in Chilham, there is a free carpark just as you turn off the main road onto Taylors Hill (postcode CT4 8BY). If you want to extend your walk, Chilham castle gardens are open to the public from 10am – 4pm Tuesdays and Thursdays from May to September. The White Horse pub in the corner of the square is a haunted 16th century inn, serving real ales, lagers, wines and spirits with a decent pub grub menu Tel: 01227 730355.

In the other corner of the square, next to Chilham castle entrance is where the walk starts (picture 1). Walk down school lane, with the school to your left until you come to Mountain Street (picture 2). Turn right and walk along the street, past Heron Manor on the left, until you come to a footpath sign on your left, between houses (picture 3).

1   2   3

At the end of the gardens, the path goes diagonally across a field (picture 4) to some steps and a stile (pictures 5 & 6).

4   5   6

Turn right and walk along the edge of the field until you reach a gate and a stile (picture 7) Walk along the edge of the next field (ignoring the first bridge over the river with a locked gate) until you reach a footbridge in the corner that crosses the river Stour (picture 8). Cross the bridge and then carefully cross the fast and busy road. Turn left and walk along to the footpath and farm shop signs (picture 9).

7   8   9

Walk up between the cottages and farm buildings, under the railway bridge and along the track (picture 10). After a few yards the path bears left up into the woodland to the left of some power lines. Carry on until you reach a kiss gate (picture 11). Further along, ignore a path that crosses left to right, but carry on until you reach a gate on the left (picture 12).

10   11   12

Walk along the path and up the steps (picture 13) until you reach a kiss gate (picture 14) and follow the well-trodden footpath across the field with spectacular views across the Kent countryside to the left, until you reach the corner of the field (picture 15).

13   14   15

Ignore the stile on the right and walk down and through a gate and a stile (picture 16), turn right and soon you will come to a track between the two fields (pictures 17 & 18).

16   17   18

This short track leads to a field. Walk diagonally across the field (picture 19) until you come to yet another stile (picture 20). Go over the stile and after a few paces you will reach a byway with several directional arrows on a post (picture 21).

19   20   21

Ignore all those directions and turn right along the track (picture 22) until you reach a fork with a marker post (picture 23). Take the left fork across some fields. Along the way, there is a memorial to Flight Lieutenant George Stoney of 501 Squadron who was shot down nearby and killed in his Hurricane 2549 on August 18th 1940 (picture 24) Lest we forget…

22   23   24

The path goes between a hedgerow (picture 25) and emerges at a cross path with two marker posts (picture 26). Walk straight ahead by the river, between houses and cross the bridge. Keep walking until you come to a level crossing (picture 27). Walk over the railway and carefully cross the busy Ashford Road onto Bagham Lane.

25   26   27

Walk past the houses on your right and turn left at the next junction (picture 28) staying on Bagham Lane and either stop for a refreshing drink in the15th century Woolpack Inn (picture 29) or carry on up to the square at the beginning of the walk.

28   29

Cobham

(3.5 miles)

This walk starts at the Ship inn, Cobham and is mainly across flat countryside and tarmac byways. If you are parking in the pub car park, please get permission from the landlord first. The pub has lots of character, with an extensive and reasonably priced menu. There are cask ale pumps on the bar (Greene King) with 10% discount per pint for CAMRA members.

The address is 14, the Street, Cobham DA12 3BN Tel: 01474 814326.

Find it on OS Explorer map 163: 68/67.

Turn left at the pub and walk down to the war memorial (picture 1). Carefully cross the busy road and walk up the byway ahead, past the houses on your right, until you reach a quaint thatched cottage next to a gate and kiss gate (pictures 2 & 3).

| 1 | 2 | 3 |

Go through the gate and stay on the path, through open fields and then a tree lined pathway (picture 4), until you reach a cattle grid and a kiss gate (picture 5). This is Cobham Park. Further along the track on "William's Hill" you will reach the Darnley Mausoleum (picture 6). The Earls of Darnley were usually buried in Westminster Abbey, but by the late 18th century, their vaults were full. In his will, the 3rd Earl, John Bligh, left instructions for a mausoleum to be built in Cobham Park, Kent, where he and his descendants could be laid to rest in a grand manner. The mausoleum was completed in 1786, at a cost of £9,000 but there was a problem… For reasons that remain unclear, possibly involving a dispute with the Bishop of Rochester, the Darnley Mausoleum was never consecrated and so could not be used for burial.

4   5   6

Carry on past the mausoleum until you reach a kiss gate (picture 7). Turn left and walk down the narrow path through woodland (picture 8). It widens before you reach yet another kiss gate (picture 8) and after a few paces ignore the path to the left and another kiss gate to the right and go straight ahead through another kiss gate (picture 9).

7   8   9

The path goes through woodland with a fence and a golf course on the left, until you reach - yes, you've guessed it - another kiss gate, with a railway track beyond (picture 10). Turn left and follow the path alongside the railway until you reach a lane (picture 11). Cross the lane and take the footpath on the opposite side (picture 12).

10   11   12

This path turns sharp right after a few paces and then continues alongside the railway, past two ponds to another kiss gate (picture 13). Turn left and when you see the sign that says Private School Grounds, (picture 14) turn right and walk across the field past the cattle trough with a yellow arrow painted on it (picture 15).

13   14   15

Continue across the field, past the marker post (picture 16), until you reach a lane (picture 17). Cross the lane and when you get to another kiss gate on the left (picture 18), ignore it and walk diagonally across the field.

16   17   18

Picture 19 shows the footpath, looking back towards the kiss gate in picture 18. Carry on through this field with sheep, until you reach the final kiss gate on the edge of the field (picture 20). Turn left and follow the path (picture 21) between the field on the left and Halfpence Lane on the right, until you emerge back at war memorial.

19 20 21

Dargate

(3 ¼ miles)

This walk is pretty flat with just a slight gradient in parts. It starts at the Dove public house in Plumpudding lane, Dargate, ME13 9HB. We did this walk on a hot Tuesday in June and unfortunately as the pub was shut for the day, we couldn't go inside and so cannot comment on the food and drinks. However, I had been there many years ago and remember that it is very quaint. Check out the menu on their website, *www.dovedargate.co.uk*. Tel: 01227 751085. Please ask permission before parking in the pub carpark.

With your back to the pub, walk along the road opposite until you reach a track next to a cottage on the left (picture 1). This track is called "Red Road" and takes you up a gradual slope through woodland. Carry on straight (ignoring any paths to the left or right); until you reach a gate to Holly Hill Farm and farm buildings (picture 2). Walk past the cottage and continue on the gravel road (picture 3).

1	2	3

Just after you reach a gate (picture 4) you will come to a fork (picture 5). Turn right and follow the track up past a house on the left and into a wood, again ignoring paths to the left and right. This path meanders through the wood. Halfway in, there is a track going off to the right (picture 6). Ignore this and bear left.

4	5	6

The path narrows here, but there are some spectacular views across the Kent countryside and the Thames estuary, with the Isle of Sheppey in the distance. When the track forks (picture 7) take the right-hand fork and follow the narrow path, with a field to the left, until you reach Crockham road (picture 8). Turn right and walk down to a road junction (picture 9).

7 8 9

Turn left and walk along until you reach a path on the right with a footpath sign (picture 10). Follow this footpath alongside an orchard, with a beech screen on your left until you reach the end of the orchard. Go through the gap in the hedge (picture 11) and continue alongside another orchard until you emerge at a lane (picture 12).

10 11 12

Turn left and walk up the lane with houses and a road called Woodlands on the right, until you see a restricted byway on the left (picture 13). Walk straight on with the cottage on your right until you reach a crossway. Take the path down towards the cottage and the road (picture 14). Turn right on the road and walk back to the pub.

13   14

Downe

(3.5 miles)

This walk is mainly cross country and crosses some quiet lanes but has some very steep hills. Try and park near the Queen's Head pub (picture above), although this little village can be very crowded, especially at weekends. This was the great naturalist Charles Darwin's Country seat and the walk takes you past Darwin house near the end, where you can purchase tickets to explore the house and grounds.

With your back to the pub, cross the road, turn right and walk along the road as if towards the camera in the picture above, until you see a footpath sign on the left (picture 1), opposite the entrance to Petleys farm (picture 2). Follow the path until it reaches a field and walk along the left hand side of the field (picture 3)…

1   2   3

…until you reach a gap in the hedge (picture 4). On the other side of the hedge there is a sign post (picture 5). Take the route for Cudham lane and pass Christmas farm on the left (picture 6), where you can take your children/ grand children to pet farm animals – another day out perhaps?

4   5   6

At the other end of the field, go through the gate (picture 7), and walk to Cudham lane keeping Christmas farm to your left and go over the stile (picture 8). At Cudham lane, turn right, walk past the carpark entrance and up onto the footpath (picture 9).

7   8   9

This path runs alongside Cudham lane, over a small track (picture 10) and emerges onto Cudham lane at picture 11. Turn right, cross the lane and turn left up the path with houses on your left (picture 12).

10   11   12

Walk along this wide path (picture 13) until you come to a sign with a bench (picture 14). Turn right and head down the steep steps (picture 15).

13   14   15

Cross the lane (picture 16) and when you reach a track (picture 17), turn right and walk back down to Cudham lane with a farm on your left (picture 18).

16   17   18

Now, the real walk should be to turn left and walk along the lane until you reach a footpath sign on the right, but there is a gap in the hedge opposite leading to a bridal way, so as a safer option, go across the lane to the bridal way and turn left, walking parallel to the lane, until you reach the sign (picture 19). With your back to the sign, you will see a stile (picture 20). Cross the stile and walk diagonally right, up the field to another stile (picture 21). We did this walk in April and this field was awash with yellow cowslips.

19   20   21

Turn left on the lane and after a short while, take the path on the left (picture 22) up and along the side of some fields (pictures 23 & 24).

22   23   24

When you reach a gate with a sign, take the path straight ahead, with the people in picture 25 until you reach a small lane (picture 26). Cross the lane and take the path opposite (picture 27).

25   26   27

The path leads between two clumps of trees (picture 28) and on past the entrance to Downe House gardens (picture 29). Go through the gate (picture 30), cross the narrow lane…

28   29   30

…and walk diagonally left down across the field (picture 31). At the bottom of the field, the path turns left for a short while and then right, through a kiss gate (picture 32) and down some steps to a sign (picture 33). Turn right and walk through the woodland, keeping the golf course to your left.

31 32 33

Walk until you reach a lane (picture 34). Cross the lane and take the path opposite with a sign to Holwood farm (picture 35) At the end of this path there is a kiss gate on the right and a sign with an arrow pointing left for a circular walk (picture 36) Ignore this sign and turn right, through the kiss gate.

34 35 36

Walk through more woodland, through a kiss gate next to a gate (picture 37) and on to another kiss gate (picture 38). The path then runs alongside a fence that separates the wood from a field and ends at the lane where the walk started (picture 39). Carefully cross the road, turn left and walk along the path to the start.

37   38   39

Eynsford

(2 miles)

Eynsford is a pretty village in North Kent, between Farningham and Shoreham, on the river Darent. There is a small car park on the right before you reach the ford and bridge (pictured above), if you are coming from the Farningham direction. There is limited parking alongside the river, opposite the pub, the Plough. If you park in the Plough's car park, please remember to book your car registration number at the bar or you will get fined. The Plough has a large restaurant and bar serving delicious meals and some real ales. Postcode: DA4 0AE Tel: 01322 862281.

With your back to the pub, turn right and walk along the road, past Home Farm and the road to the right, until you reach a footpath sign on the right (picture 1). Walk across the field until you reach a pedestrian level crossing (picture 2). Carefully cross the rails and continue along the well-trodden path (picture 3).

1	2	3

Go through the gap in the hedge (picture 4) and carry on until you reach a lane (picture 5). This lane leads to Eagle Heights Wild Life foundation where you can watch daily flying displays. There also lots of other animals to see, plus a cafeteria.

Back to the walk... cross the lane and walk across the field (picture 6).

4	5	6

When you reach a track (picture 7), turn left and continue down until you reach a gap on the right (picture 8). Walk down through the wood until you reach a lane with Lullingstone Roman Villa on the left (picture 9). This villa first started life in 100AD and continued to expand until the 4th century. Well worth a visit.

7   8   9

Walk past the Villa and continue up the lane, under the viaduct, back to the start and perhaps a refreshing drink in the Plough!

Looking back towards Eynsford and the viaduct from the walk.

Fawkham Green

(2.8 miles)

Circular walk from the Rising Sun

The Rising Sun is situated on the village green about ¼ mile from Brands Hatch race circuit, with an open log fire, oak beams, real ales and a restaurant serving home cooked food. They also have B&B with a four-poster bed in one room, so what is there not to like? The walk starts from the green. Parking at the pub is limited and so cars sometimes overflow into the road opposite. This walk is a mix of fields, woodlands and mostly quiet country lanes. If you are lucky, you may see the odd Spitfire or Hurricane as they are quite often flying overhead on flights from their base at nearby Biggin Hill.

Rising Sun Postcode: DA3 8NL Tel: 01474 872291.

With your back to the pub, turn left and walk along the road for a few yards until you reach Michaels Lane on the right (picture 1) Walk with caution as this road can be quite busy. Walk up Michaels Lane until you reach a slight bend with a footpath ascending in a field on the left (picture 2).

Follow the footpath across the field and into the woods (picture 3).

1   2   3

As you continue through the woods, you can see a wooden "village" to the right that someone has meticulously built, with several wooden bivouacs and even a fire pit. (Pictures 4 & 5). Continue up until you enter a field (picture 6).

4   5   6

and follow the path diagonally across and then along between houses to emerge on Manor Lane (picture 7). Cross the road and continue onto the road leading to Redlibbets Golf Clubhouse.

Just before the clubhouse, follow the road down to the lake and off to the left, following the marker posts, (pictures 8 & 9)…

7   8   9 – looking back to
                              the lake and club

…until you reach the edge of the golf course (picture 10). **Be very wary of golf balls whilst crossing the fairways!** Walk ahead through the short woodland with overhead power lines and emerge onto a field of horses (picture 11).

Follow the path around the perimeter of the field, through a gate (picture 12).

10   11   12

Walk to another gate in the corner (picture 13). Go through the gate and turn right, walking through Chapel wood, until you reach Chapel wood road (picture 14). Cross over the road with care (fast moving cars) and turn right and walk along the pavement for about 500 yards until you reach Butchers Lane on the right (picture 15).

13   14   15

Cross over the road again and walk along Butchers Lane to the end, where it meets Manor Lane (picture 16) and turn right. After you pass the Redlibbets entrance on the right and Manns farm and West Yoke Farm on the left, take the road on the left – which is Michaels Lane (picture 17). Walk down this very narrow, but quiet lane back to the start and a nice pint of something refreshing!

16   17

Fordcombe

(3.5 miles)

This walk is mainly flat with a steep incline at the end. Part of it is along the meandering upper river Medway. We visited in late April when the fields were awash with yellow rape, the woodlands with bluebells and gambolling lambs in a field in part of the walk along the river.

The walk starts when you park in or near the Chafford Arms. Postcode for the pub is TN3 0SA Telephone: 01892 740267. If you chose to park in the pub carpark, please check with the landlord first. They serve excellent meals and real ales, with great views of the surrounding countryside from the rear garden.

With your back to the pub, turn left and walk up the village, past the junction with Broad Lane until you reach a footpath sign on the right (picture 1). Walk across the cricket field to a gap in the left-hand corner (picture 2). Carry on past the fields until you reach a gate (picture 3).

1   2   3

Continue on until you reach a stile with a house on the left (picture 4) and then Broad Lane. Cross the lane to the footpath through the woods (picture 5) until it emerges onto a field. Walk along the edge of the field with a steep drop on the left (picture 6).

4   5   6

When you reach a post (picture 7), there are two options. For the true path, turn right then left and the path runs along the edge of the field to a footbridge (picture 8). However, if you walk straight across from picture 7 and into the woods, there is a picturesque woodland walk alongside a gentle stream. You will need to negotiate the narrow stream at the end. When you re-join the true path, carry on across the field and the alongside another field (picture 9).

7   8   9

Eventually you will reach a stile and a lane (picture 10). Turn left on the lane and walk down to a bridge over the river Medway (picture 11). Walk over the bridge and take the signed footpath on the right, along the side of the river until you reach a gate and a stile (picture 12).

10   11   12

Carry on to another gate and a stile (picture 13) and after a short while you will come to a footbridge over the river (picture 14), cross the bridge and a field to gate leading to a lane (picture 15).

13   14   15

Cross the lane and take the signed path (picture 16), across the small field to a kiss gate (picture 17) and continue until you reach a footbridge on your right (picture 18) Cross the bridge and walk up the steep field.

16   17   18

At the top it turns left and then into a woodland path (picture 19). Continue through the wood until you reach a gate (picture 20). DO NOT go through this gate, but turn right and follow the path up, with a small stream on the left. The path emerges into a field. The walk is quite steep here, but carry on up, ignoring the path on the left as it turns at the top. Stop, catch your breath and admire the amazing view. The path is quite straightforward from here on, until your reach the back gardens of some houses and the Chafford Arms. Walk along the rear of the gardens until you reach a track on the right that leads you back to the village. Turn right and head back to the pub for a refreshing drink.

19

20

Fordwich

(3.5 miles)

Fordwich is a very quaint and picturesque village on the banks of the river Stour, where you can hire Kayaks and paddle boards. There many walks along the river, but this one takes you inland. Parts of the walk are very narrow and overgrown. This walk starts at the George & Dragon pub, right next to the river Stour, postcode CT2 0DB, Tel: 01227 710661. The pub has a large car park opposite, but it gets very busy, so get there early. If there is no room, go over the bridge and take the second right into Marlow Meadows, where you should find a few spaces.

With your back to the car park, turn right and walk along to King Street (picture 1). When the road turn right, carefully cross the road and go straight ahead towards the Fordwich Arms (picture 2). This pub is now a high-end Michelin restaurant. Turn right and walk along the street... (picture 3).

1	2	3

…Until you reach School Lane (picture 4). Follow the path through two kiss gates (pictures 5 & 6).

4	5	6

Keep going straight ahead when you see the sign markers, ignoring any cross paths (pictures 7 & 8). Eventually you will come to a narrow path on the right (picture 9) If you reach a wide, rutted track, you have gone too far.

7	8	9

This path was very overgrown when we walked there (October), but persevere and you will eventually emerge onto Stodmarsh Road (picture 10). Turn right and after about 30 yards, you will see a path with two logs across the entrance and a partly obscured footpath sign on the left (picture 11). Walk along this path until you reach a large Beech tree on the right – turn right here and follow the path (picture 12).

10   11   12

When you come to a junction (pictures 13 & 14), keep taking the right forks and you will pass an open field fenced off on the right. Keep going, through a logging area, until you reach a gate, back to Stodmarsh Road (picture 15).

13   14   15

Turn left and carefully walk along the road, past a bungalow on the left, until you see a car park sign on the right (picture 16). Go through the gap and walk across the playing fields and you will see a wooden gate and a stile a little to the left of it (picture 17). Go over the stile and follow the path, The path narrows as it goes down the right-hand side of horses' fields and then through a copse. Keep to the left of the marker post (picture 18).

16   17   18

Eventually you come to a dilapidated stile (picture 19) that leads to a path across a field, with the church spire in the background (picture 20). Go through the kiss gate (picture 21).

19   20   21

And then another kiss gate (picture 22), to a path between houses that leads to Spring Lane. At the end, turn right onto the High Street (picture 23) and retrace your steps back to the start.

22   23

Higham

(4.5 miles)

If you like making sloe gin, then a walk here in mid-September will supply you with sloes in abundance, especially along the canal road and between pictures 5-7. For parking, if you use the postcode ME3 7JQ the SatNav it will take you to Higham station, just take the next right and park where you can. The start of the walk is on the corner of canal road. There used to be a pub on the corner, but alas it has been converted to houses (see picture 1).

The first part of this walk is on the canal road alongside the disused Thames & Medway canal. This a quiet road with speed bumps to discourage the occasional racer, but we found it to be used more by cyclists. Halfway along canal road there is a monument on what used to be the other bank of the canal, with an information board (picture 2). After the railway bridge (picture 3), turn immediately right.

1   2   3

As you approach the gates to the business there, you will see a footpath on the right (picture 4). Follow the path up some steps and along the path, through a gate (picture 5) until you reach a pedestrian level crossing (picture 6).

| 4 | 5 | 6 |

Follow the path over a wooden bridge (picture 7), a gate (picture 8) and past some houses until you emerge at Church Street (picture 9).

| 7 | 8 | 9 |

Take the footpath opposite across a field with houses to the left (picture 10). On the opposite side of the field, the path narrows to a stone path between two ditches (picture 11). Carry on into an enormous field, along a track, past Oakleigh Manor and large pond and Oakleigh Lodge on the left and farm buildings further along to the right, until you come to Buckland Road (picture 12).

10   11   12

On the opposite side of the road is a footpath sign – DO NOT use this path, but turn right along the road and after a few yards you will see another path and wooden bridge on the left (picture 13). Go through the hedge, cross over the track and go through the metal gate (picture 14). Walk diagonally right to two further wooden gates across more fields (picture 15).

13   14   15

Go through another wooden kiss gate (picture 16) and across a field that leads to a metal kiss gate (picture 17) and Lillechurch Road. Cross the road and take the path up the hill (picture 18).

16   17   18

This is a straight path across open land to Lower Rochester Road. Walk across the road to the next path (pictures 19 & 20). After a short while, the path splits (picture 21).

19   20   21

Turn right across the open fields towards White house farm (picture 22). When you reach the small road (picture 23), turn right and about 20 yards along just past some trees, you will see two paths on the left (see picture 24). Take the path to the left along the side of the field and soon you will emerge onto Chequers Street at the start of the walk.

22   23   24

Horton Kirby

(4.6 miles)

This walk is mainly across country and crosses some quiet lanes but has some quite steep footpaths. Try to park along "The Street" near the Fighting Cocks pub (picture above), although this little village can be very crowded, especially at weekends. If you are intending to eat or drink in the pub after the walk, then park in the carpark and inform the landlords beforehand. Their telephone number is 01322 862299 postcode DA4 9BY. The pub has an extensive garden down to the river Darent, with a children's' play area.

With your back to the pub, turn left and walk along The Street and around the bend, past the church and Court Lodge cottages until you come to the junction with Jacob's Lane on the right (picture 1). Cross the road, enter the field through the kiss gate and follow the well-marked footpath (picture 2). At the top, the walk crosses "Skinny Lane" (picture 3).

1   2   3

Follow the path to a kiss gate in a hedgerow (picture 4). Go through the gate and walk diagonally right, across the field (picture 5), until you reach another kiss gate in a hedgerow (picture 6).

4   5   6

The walk takes you through two more kiss gates (pictures 7 & 8) to Rabbits Road. Cross the road and go straight across the field (picture 9)…

7   8   9

…to the railway bridge (picture 10). Turn right after the bridge and follow the path along the side of a coppiced screen of trees (picture 11) to Gill's Farm. Walk straight ahead between the farm buildings until you reach Gill's Road (picture 12).

10   11   12

Cross Gill's Road and follow the path straight ahead towards a line of trees, ignoring the path that bears left (picture 13), until you come to a post with three arrows on it (picture 14). Turn left and take the path towards the farm buildings of St. Margaret's farm (picture 15).

13   14   15

Walk straight ahead between the farm buildings until you come to St. Margaret's Road (picture 16). Cross the road and walk between two hedgerows and eventually you will see a concrete footpath sign (picture 17) and then after a few more steps, the hedgerow ends and there are 360^0 panoramic views over the country side. Carry on to another gap in a hedgerow (picture 18) across another field.

16   17   18

Where the footpath meets another coming from the right (picture 19), turn left down the steps to Roman Villa Road. Turn right and walk along for about fifty metres to a footpath sign on the left leading down across a field (picture 20). At the bottom of the field, cross the lane and go through a gap between a wall and a hedge (picture 21).

19   20   21

Go through the gate to the church (picture 22) and walk through the graveyard to the main gate (picture 23). Turn left onto the road and walk past a couple of cottages to the entrance to a distribution centre (picture 24).

22   23   24

Turn left into the site entrance and walk until you see a sign for Darenth Fishing, with a narrow footpath to the left (picture 25). Walk along this path between the fishery and the distributions centre and then up some steps (picture 26). When you reach the field, walk diagonally across (picture 27). This part of the walk from picture 24, is part of the Darenth Valley path which follows the river Darent to Eynsford and beyond.

25   26   27

At the end of the field, walk along the gravel path (picture 28) and eventually you will reach Homesdale Hill (picture 29). Turn right and follow the road beside the river, through South Darenth village, under the railway viaduct and past the village hall, all the way back to the start.

28   29

Hythe

(5 miles)

Circular walk along the front and the Royal Military canal

The walk starts from the Imperial Hotel on the sea front at Princes Parade, Hythe. Postcode CT21 6AE.

Opposite the hotel is pay and display parking (picture 1). This is a gentle walk on the flat and level, with no muddy boots! Stand at the seafront and turn left, following the concrete sea defences for about 1 ½ miles (picture 2) until you come to the start of the Royal Military canal across the road (picture 3).

| 1 | 2 – looking back to the start | 3 |

Carefully cross the road and walk around the end of the canal to the other side (picture 4). Walk along the pavement towards the house on the right in picture 4, until you see a track that leads down to the canal, just before that first house. Take this track down to the canal and keeping the canal to your left, walk along the byway (picture 5). There are three footbridges across the canal along this route. Continue until you reach the road that leads to the Imperial Hotel and cross over the road. The path becomes more permanent from here (picture 6). Carry on until the canal does a sharp right. Here you will see a path across a playing field. This leads to roads that eventually lead to the local fire station and an alleyway that leads to the sea front. On the right are two Martello towers (picture 7)…

| 4 | 5 | 6 |

…and to the left a café (picture 8). Turn left on the beach and walk a few yards to the sea wall. Walk along the seafront (picture 9), back to the start.

8   9

Ide Hill

(4 ¾ miles)

Circular walk from the community shop

If there is room, you can park at the Community Shop (we arrived on a Sunday and there were plenty of spaces) otherwise park safely somewhere close by. If you prefer to go up to the village green and park, you will see the Cock inn, perhaps a welcome stop for refreshment after the walk? However, when I re-visited this walk in January, the track after picture 3 was impassable as there was coppicing work being carried out and the track had been churned up with thick, deep mud by heavy machinery. Maybe this would best as a summer walk?

Walk back up and away from the shop towards the large house on the road (picture 1) and cross the road at the footpath sign. Be very careful as this is quite a fast road. Once safely across the road, take the ramp to the left of the track (picture 2). After a short walk you will come to a forked path with a gate to the left (picture 3).

| 1 | 2 | 3 |

Ignore the small path on the right-hand side and go around the gate and follow the path to another fork in the path (picture 4). You can see from the picture that the post with yellow markers is further along the path than the fork, which is misleading. Take the right fork down the hill through the woods until you come to a small road (pictures 5 & 6). Ignore those signs and walk down the road to the end.

| 4 | 5 | 6 |

Here you will see a footpath on the left (ignore another a few steps on, to the left of two garages) until you come to a narrow path between a field and woodland (picture 7). Follow this path as it stretches out across fields and woodland to a small bridge over a stream (pictures 8-11). The path eventually finishes at a stile that takes you through someone's back garden to a lane (picture 12).

7   8   9

10   11   12

Turn right onto the lane and keep right at the next junction (picture 13), down to the bottom of the hill where you will see a sign post for a path on the left. Take this path alongside the stream until you come to a footbridge (picture 14). Follow the path until you reach another lane (picture 15).

13   14   15

Turn left onto this lane and after a few steps, you will see a footpath sign on the right, together with a sign for Bough Beech Oast house (picture 16). This lane leads to the oast house, where you can picnic if you so desire and watch the waterfowl on the lakes. Go past the oast house on the right-hand side until you reach a kiss gate (picture 17). Keep to the right, along the edge of the field, until you reach a fork with two gate and yellow arrows (picture 18).

16   17   18

Take the right-hand gate. Follow this path through two more gates and a stile (pictures 19-21), where you will emerge onto a lane.

19   20   21

Turn right onto this lane and walk until you come to a junction. The footpath is on the other side of the road (picture 22), but be very careful when crossing this junction as the cars appear from nowhere. Whilst we were there, there was a car up the bank that had not made the bend and an ambulance was in attendance. Be warned! Follow the path as it meanders through woodland, over a footbridge and through fields until you reach a tarmac bridleway next to farm buildings. Turn right and walk up the bridleway until you reach a fast road (pictures 23 – 25).

22   23   24

Carefully cross the road and turn left. Walk along the road until you see a footpath sign, just after the second house on the other side of the road (picture 26). Cross this field until you come to two gates, one either end of a footbridge (picture 27).

25   26   27

There were sheep in this and the next field when we walked. On the other side of the second field, go through the kiss gate and up the steps (picture 28) to a lane and turn left. Follow this lane to the start of your walk.

28

Knockholt Station Circular Walk

(5 miles)

If you are arriving by car, there is pay parking along London Road, which is free on weekends and bank holidays. The station postcode is TN14 7HR. This walk has some steep and challenging inclines. If you are doing this walk in the summer, shorts are not advisable, as part of the walk has a very narrow path with high stinging nettles.

Almost opposite the station is a clearly marked footpath and kiss gate (picture 1). Go through and walk up the incline (picture 2). When you come to a footpath sign, go straight ahead on the well-marked path, with a disused carpark (picture 3). This was the carpark for the now defunct Broke Hill golf club.

| 1 | 2 | 3 |

Keep walking until you reach another kiss gate and go through (picture 4) when you reach a fork (picture 5) take the left-hand fork to Stone house Lane (picture 6).

| 4 | 5 | 6 |

Turn left and walk along the lane until you reach a gate on the right (picture 7). Go through the gate and immediately turn left and walk keeping the hedge on your right (picture 8) until you reach a stile with a footpath sign beyond (picture 9).

7   8   9

Ignore the sign's directions and take the path to the right (picture 10). This leads through the woods (picture 11) and eventually opens up into a field, part of another disused golf club. Walk up the field until you reach a footpath on the right with a post and a yellow arrow (picture 12).

10   11   12

Walk along the path, over the stile (picture 13) until you reach another stile (picture 14). Continue walking alongside Coolings' nursery until you come to Rushmore Hill. Carefully cross the road and take the fork down Hookwood Road (picture 15).

13   14   15

After a short walk, take the footpath on the left (picture 16) and when you reach a gate with a stile to the right (picture 17) go over the stile and walk down the field, keeping the dilapidated fence to your left, until you reach another stile that leads into woods (picture 18).

16   17   18

Walk up the steep path through the woods until you reach a stile (picture 19). The footpath turns left here. Eventually you will come to yet another stile that leads onto Perrys Lane (picture 20). Turn right and walk until you reach the junction of Washneys Road and Fairtrough Road (picture 21) Turn left onto Washneys Road.

19   20   21

As the road bears to the left, there is signpost and path to Pratts Bottom (pictures 22 & 23). The first part of this path is very narrow with high stinging nettles on both sides during the summer months – not advisable for bare legs! It then opens up and after walking through woodland, you will eventually reach a gate (picture 24). Cross the road and take the gate opposite.

22   23   24

Turn right in the field and walk up to a gate (picture 25). Turn left onto the path and walk along, until you reach a byeway and eventually you will emerge at Pratts Bottom village green. Walk across the green and take the footpath beside the Bull's head car park with a sign stating 1½ miles to Chelsfield (picture 26). This is a steep, stepped path. At the top you come to a fork (picture 27). Go over the stile on the right.

25   26   27

After a few paces, you come to a stile on the left (picture 28). Go over the stile and walk diagonally across the field until you reach a stile leading into the woods (picture 29). Ignore the cross path and continue to walk up the path through the woods until you reach a field (picture 30).

28   29   30

This path leads you to Stonehouse Lane (picture 31) cross the lane, go through the kiss gate and follow the path along the edge of the field until you come to a fork (picture 32). Turn right and cross the field with the trees to your left and continue until you reach the footpath that you were originally on, just before picture 4. Turn left and retrace your steps back to Knockholt station.

31   32

Lenham

(4 miles)

The walk starts just outside Lenham at the Wishful Thinker pub, postcode ME17 2HY. The pub is like the Dr. Who Tardis – enormous once you step inside, plus a massive garden, as well secluded dining areas and also B&B. The car park extends considerably, allowing for around 200 cars.

With your back to the pub, turn left and walk a few yards to the junction and turn right (picture 1). Walk over the bridge spanning the M20 and take the footpath immediately on the left (picture 2). Follow this path over stiles, hugging the side of the wood until you come to a fork (picture 3) Take the right-hand fork.

1   2   3

The path is not defined here, so head for the trees (picture 4) and follow the field, when you will see a lake with Chilston Park Hotel on the other side (picture 5). Soon you will come to a gate with a lane (picture 6).

4   5   6

The gate has a yellow arrow on it (picture 7). Go through the gate and then take the stile on the left (pictures 8). Walk diagonally left across the field towards the Lime trees (picture 9).

7   8   9

Go over the stile (picture 10 and head for some low voltage pylons and then a house on the right, until you come to a gate (picture 11). If you look up the drive of the house you will see a footpath sign (picture 12).

10   11   12

Go over the stile and head diagonally across the field toward the tree line (picture 13). Follow the field along the edge until you come to yellow arrow post to the right of a gap (picture 14). Follow the sign to a kiss gate on to a lane (picture 15).

13   14   15

Turn right on the lane and walk up the hill until you come to a three headed footpath sign (picture 16). Take the path that points across the lane on to a field (picture 17) until you come to a kiss gate with a warning sign stating to keep dogs on a lead (picture 18).

16   17   18

Walk on to another kiss gate (picture 19) cross another field (picture 20) to yet another kiss gate (picture 21).

19   20   21

Walk over the narrow wooden footbridge (picture 22) keep to the left of the field (picture 23), to a stile and on to a lane (picture 24). Turn right on the lane and walk back over the M20 to the start.

22   23   24

Meopham

(5.5 miles)

This walk starts at Meopham green. There are two pubs nearby, the Cricketers Inn DA13 0QA (by the windmill in the picture above) and the Kings Arms DA13 0QB (to the left of the green out of shot). Both offer real ales and home cooked food.

This is a hilly walk over fields and through woodlands with some steep climbs. There are many kiss gates and stiles on this walk, so not all are shown. Allow 2 ½ – 3 hours.

At the corner of the green there is a memorial stone. Turn your back to the stone and you will see a track, which is the start of the walk (see picture 1). Walk along this path and through a kiss gate (picture 2), until you reach another kiss gate on the left (picture 3). Turn left here and walk down diagonally to another kiss gate and through to a quiet lane.

1   2   3

Take the path on the opposite side of the lane, until you reach two gates (picture 4). Keep going straight ahead across a long field until you reach another gate and a quiet lane (picture 5).

4   5

Almost immediately right, there is an old stone footpath sign (picture 6) that leads up towards a house. Walk diagonally across the field with the rugby goalpost, until you reach an opening into the woods. Follow this path until it emerges through a kiss gate onto a byway (picture 7). A little way along this byway, the path splits 3-ways. Ignore a kiss gate on the left and the byway to the right and take the path straight ahead (picture 8).

6   7   8

When you come to a road, go over the stile on the other side of the road (picture 9) and continue until you reach a lane with a tennis court opposite (picture 10). Cross the lane, go over the stile and walk up the side of tennis court to the wood, where there is a stile next to a gate. Go over the stile. The path is very narrow here but quickly widens. This part of the walk is very steep and you may want an excuse to catch your breath by stopping hallway up and turning to admire the view! This will eventually bring you to a converted barn on the left (picture 11) and the pretty Combe Hill farm cottage on the right.

9   10   11

Turn left on the lane and in a short while you will come to a stile and a path on the left (picture 12). Follow the path over another stile, through a gate into woodland and yet another stile until you reach a wide path between two paddocks with horses (picture 13). Walk to the bottom of the paddock, turn right and walk to a stile on the left (picture 14).

12　　　　　　　　　　13　　　　　　　　　　14

This leads to another stile onto a lane (picture 15). Turn right and after a short while, turn left over a stile at a sign posted walk (picture 16). Follow this well signposted walk over stiles and through kiss gates until just before you reach a lane, there is path with a blue arrow on the right (picture 17). Walk up this path to a road and cross to a stile on the opposite side of the road. Walk diagonally right, across the field to a gate.

15　　　　　　　　　　16　　　　　　　　　　17

Follow this path through a gate (the path is fenced here) and then yet another stile until you reach a stile at St. Bernards and Dean Lane (picture 18). Take the signposted path (picture 19) until you emerge at another lane (picture 20).

18   19   20

Turn right and almost immediately turn left through a gate (picture 21) and walk along the edge of a field until you reach David Street. Turn right and find the signpost on the left (picture 22). Carry on over the stile (picture 23)…

21   22   23

…and to the top of a field (picture 24). Walk left diagonally down to the corner of the field to a kiss gate with a sign marked NS265 (picture 25). Go up the side of the wood to another kiss gate (picture 26).

24   25   26

You will eventually emerge at the top of a hill with a path traversing right diagonally across a field (picture 27) and up the other side. Go through a kiss gate and walk along the byway until you reach a footpath on the right (picture 28) walk past a small allotment on the left (picture 29).

27   28   29

Cross a field to another stile (picture 30) leading back on the byway. Walk along this byway back to the start.

30

Offham

(4 miles)

On the village green at Offham is an old Quintain, better known as the "Tilt", where romans first practised their horsemanship. This was later used for practice by jousting knights. The idea was to hit the tilt as hard and fast as you were able, so that the weight (usually a bag of sand) at the other end flew high and missed the rider as he passed underneath. This is where the expression "To go at it full tilt" originated. You can park along the main road, perhaps outside the Kings Arms pub. where you can enjoy a meal and refreshments after. Postcode ME19 5NR. Tel: 01732 870114 OS Explorer map No. 148, 57/65.

From the pub, walk left past the village green to Tower hill and turn right (picture 1). Continue along the lane, passing a stone footpath sign on the right (picture 2) and through the gate at Kentfield House (picture 3).

1   2   3

Carry on straight on, through the next two gates (pictures 4 & 5) until you reach a footpath diversion sign (picture 6).

4   5   6

This footpath was diverted to make way for a quarry. Follow the track through the woods (picture 7) until you reach a track on the left (picture 8). This track leads back up to the original footpath. However, if you carry on straight ahead instead, you will reach the original footpath further along (picture 9).

7   8   9

We opted to take the longest route and turned left at picture 8, which eventually led to a kiss gate (picture 10). This route proved to be a mistake, as the path was completely waterlogged after a long period of rain, so unless the weather has been dry for a few weeks, I recommend that you take the shorter route straight ahead to picture 9. Whichever route you take, turn right and walk along the long straight track known as Lord's Walk, ignoring all crossing footpaths (picture 11), past some cottages, until you reach Comp Road. Take the unmarked track on the opposite side of the road (picture 12).

10   11   12

Walk along the track, ignoring the track to the right until you see a footpath marker post (picture 13) Follow this path around the edge of the field until you come to a water tank (picture 14). Follow the track until it forks at some fruit pickers' accommodation and take the track straight ahead (picture 15).

13   14   15

Bear right at the marker post (picture 16) and on through the gate (picture 17) until you reach the road (picture 18). Walk along this road, back to the start.

16   17   18

Oxted

(4 miles)

The walk starts at the Royal Oak pub, (postcode RH8 0RR) It has extensive seating with a unique menu and real local ales. Technically, this is in Surrey, not Kent, but a lovely walk nonetheless.

Cross the road and enter the woods via the kiss gate (picture 1). Just past the gate there is a notice that explains that the woods were used as an ammunition dump during World War two. When you get to a fork in the path (picture 2), take the left-hand fork and again, take the left hand fork a little further on (picture 3).

| 1 | 2 | 3 |

Go through the narrow gap in the fence (picture 4) and turn right at the gate (picture 5). When you reach Merle common road, turn left (picture 6)…

| 4 | 5 | 6 |

…Walk past a house called "Little Earls" until you see a footpath sign on the opposite of the road (picture 7). Don't follow the path that the arrow shows, but walk straight ahead, past the houses and eventually you will emerge at Red Lane, next to a grand house (picture 8). Cross the lane and enter the wood by the footpath sign (picture 9).

7   8   9

When you reach a stile (picture 10), go over the stile and head diagonally right across the field (picture 11) to another stile (picture 12).

10   11   12

After the stile, take the left-hand fork and walk through the woods and eventually you will emerge onto Grants Lane (picture 13). Turn left and walk along to Comforts Cottage, next to which there is a footpath sign to a path alongside (picture 14). Walk along the narrow path to a stile (picture 15).

13   14   15

Turn right and walk along the edge of the field with a wall to your right, to another stile (picture 16). The footpath was non-existent when we visited in November, but head for the bottom left-hand corner of the field to a gap (picture 17) that leads to a stile and a wooden bridge over the crooked river (picture 18).

16   17   18

After a few paces, cross the stile (picture 19) and walk up the footpath alongside a row of trees until you come to a railway crossing point (picture 20). Carry on past this and along the path with the trees to your left until you reach a kiss gate (picture 21).

19   20   21

Go through another gate (picture 22) and walk until you come to a kiss gate that leads to Monks Lane (picture 23). Turn right and walk down the lane until you reach a junction with Grants Lane (picture 24). Cross the lane and enter Stafford Wood.

22   23   24

Go past the carpark on the left; ignore the cross paths and walk straight ahead on the wide path. When you see a gate ahead, walk across the wide cross path and take the narrow path to the right of the gate (picture 25). When you reach the pond (picture 26), turn left and after a few paces you will see a post with an arrow pointing right. Take this path (picture 27).

25   26   27

When you come to Dwelly Lane, walk across the lane to another footpath (picture 28), then over a stile (picture 29) and follow the path between a hedge and a field to a gate (picture 30).

28   29   30

After the gate, walk diagonally right (picture 31) to a stile, with the rear of the Royal Oak pub in the distance (picture 32). Follow the path around the right-hand side of the field, past the pub to a gate (picture 33). Go through the gate, turn right and walk back to the start.

31   32   33

Riverhead, Sevenoaks

(4 miles)

This walk is mainly through woodlands with gradual uphill gradients. The walk starts in Dibden Lane, Sevenoaks. The only postcode is for the nearby farm TN14 6BT, so use this and then carry on along the lane until you reach the road bridge and park along there. (OS explorer map 147 – 52/54).

Walk back until you reach a kiss gate and a gate (picture 1). Go through the gate and turn left. You are now in the Montreal estate. This is quite a long uphill gradient on a wide track with coppicing on both sides. Apparently, this track was used during the build up to the D-day landings to conceal many armoured vehicles from German reconnaissance planes. When you reach a kiss gate (picture 2), go through, cross the lane and carry on straight ahead. If you look to your left, you will see a circular construction which was probably for an anti-aircraft battery. When you come to another lane, turn right (picture 3).

| 1 | 2 | 3 |

When you reach a junction (picture 4), turn left and walk along until you see a gate and kiss gate on the right (picture 5). Go through the gate and follow the path straight ahead, past a footpath signpost (picture 6).

| 4 | 5 | 6 |

Take the left fork through the woods (picture 7), until you come to a path on the right with an unused kiss gate and yellow arrow on a post. Take this path (pictures 8 & 9).

7   8   9

Keep walking straight ahead, past the arrow post (picture 10), down the slope and turn right (picture 11) You should now be walking to the left of a small brook. When you reach a post with four yellow arrows (picture 12), you can turn right. However, when we were there, it was very overgrown with stinging nettles and so we carried on straight…

10   11   12

…walked past the bushes and then turned right (picture 13). This leads you to a kiss gate (picture 14). If you had taken the first option, you would have arrived at the same place from the right. After a few paces, cross the bridge (picture 15).

13   14   15

After going uphill for a few yards, you will see a fork with a large oak tree in the middle (picture 16). Take the right fork and carry on, with the fenced off coppice on your right and a yellow arrow marker post (picture 17). Go through the last kiss gate (picture 18) and carry on walking back to the start.

16   17   18

Shipbourne No. 1

(3.4 miles)

There is a pub nearby called the Chaser Inn and the carpark gets very busy, but there is a lane opposite with lots of parking space. (Picture 1) The pub has an extensive menu and real ales.

Postcode: TN11 9PE. Tel: 01732 810360.

Walk along the lane that leads to Shipbourne (picture 2) and continue along until the lane bears right and there is a narrow path between the houses (picture 3) the signpost is there, but hidden amongst the shrubbery. There was a car parked over the entrance, possibly to deter walkers?

1   2   3

At the end of the narrow path there is a kiss gate that leads to an open field (pictures 4 & 5). Follow this path to Fairlawne Home Farm. We travelled in November, when there were many bunches of mistletoe visible in the trees.

4   5

Just after the farm, there is cattle grid (picture 6) with a gate on one side and a stile on the other. Continue to a lane and cross over to go over a stile (picture 7).

6   7

Follow the path over a stile and a small stream (pictures 8 & 9), until you come to another stile (picture 10).

8   9   10

DO NOT go over this stile, but turn left and follow the path across the field (picture 11) At the other side of the field there are two stiles, one each side of a narrow woodland (pictures 12 & 13).

11   12   13

After traversing the second stile, follow the path as it goes ahead to a tree and then turns left, heading for another stile to a quiet lane (picture 14). Turn right and after a few paces, turn left and go through the gate (picture 15) and follow the path until you reach a cross path with a yellow post (picture 16).

14   15   16

Turn left and follow the path, down to a lake (picture 17). Turn left on the road and walk past buildings until you come to another gate (picture 18) Follow the path over a small stream (picture 19) and walk up to a narrow path between the houses on the left of the field. Now you are back at Shipbourne.

17   18   19

Shipbourne No. 2

(3.4 miles)

This walk starts from the church next to the Chaser inn as in Shipbourne walk No 1. Parking is in the lane opposite with lots of parking space. However, this area attracts lots of walkers, so it would be advisable to get there early.

Walk through the church grounds to the kiss gate at the rear (picture 1) and turn left. After a short while you will see a post with yellow arrows (picture 2). Turn right diagonally across the field (picture 3)...

1   2   3

...until you reach a stream and a gap (picture 4). Ignore the path to the left (this is where you return), but head for the corner of the wood in the distance. This path is not very well defined. You should find a pond in the woods on the corner (picture 5). Head straight for the gap in the trees ahead of you (picture 6).

4   5   6

You will come to a track to the left and a post with yellow arrows (picture 7). Do not take the track, but carry on straight ahead until you reach a stile onto a lane with a stile on the other side of the lane (pictures 8 & 9).

7   8   9

Go over the second stile into the field to yet another stile by a gate (picture 10), then a sign by a track (picture 11). Cross the track and carry on until you reach a redundant stile with an opening into the field next to it (picture 12). Use the stile if you wish, but it's easier to use the gap! Carry on straight ahead.

10   11   12

The path narrows by a fence (picture 13) and you eventually emerge onto a lane (picture 14). Turn left and walk along the lane, past houses, until you reach a lane with a sign (picture 15) and a pond on the opposite side of the road. Turn left, up the lane.

13   14   15

There are private houses along this lane. Ignore the sign post on the right (picture 16) and continue up the lane until it bears left (picture 17). Take the path straight ahead until you reach another stile (picture 18).

16	17	18

Carry on, over a stile and a bridge (picture 19), another stile to a narrow path (picture 20) and yet another stile, into a wood (picture 21).

19	20	21

When you reach a lane (picture 22), turn left and after a few yards turn right onto a signposted path (picture 23). When you reach a gate with a narrow path to the right (picture 24), do not take this path, but turn left.

22   23   24

When you reach a very fast road (picture 25), carefully cross over and turn right. After a few yards turn left onto the footpath (picture 26) and over the field (picture 27) which takes you back the stream in picture 5. Go through the gap and back up the path to the church.

25   26   27

St. Margaret's Bay

(4.5 miles)

The walk starts at the end of a road, at the Dover Patrol Memorial, Postcode CT15 6DS. This monument is dedicated to the sailors of the Royal Navy and the Merchant Navy, who lost their lives patrolling the Dover straits during the two world wars. There are several parking spaces opposite the monument, but this is a busy spot for walkers, so get there early to ensure you get a spot. The first part of this walk along the white cliffs can be very bracing with a stiff sea breeze, so remember to dress accordingly. There are a couple of uphill paths in the second half.

With your back to the monument and facing the sea, turn left and go through the kiss gate (picture 1) Follow the well-trodden path along the cliffs and eventually you will come to a golf course on the left and houses (picture 2) and a view of a small beach called "The Swamp" on the right (picture 3).

1   2   3

At the end of this path, descend a flight of steps (picture 4) to emerge at Old Stairs Bay (picture 5) Turn left and walk up Old Stairs Road (picture 6).

4   5   6

When you come to fork in the road (picture 7), if you look to your right, you will see a narrow track (picture 8). This is the unadopted part of Queens Down Road. Walk up this road until you reach a crossroads (picture 9).

7   8   9

At the crossroads, turn left and walk along Northcote Road, which eventually bends to the right and uphill. This is now Bayview Road. This road becomes just a track, but carry on up until you reach a T junction (picture 10). Turn left, walk along the road (picture 11) and after a few paces, you will see a path on the left, running diagonally across an open field (picture 12).

10   11   12

Continue along this well-defined path, with a line of trees to the left, with views of the golf course between the gaps, until you reach an open field with a path running diagonally down to a gap between the hedge, leading onto a road (pictures 13 & 14) Alternatively, you can turn left at picture 13 and walk down to the lane (picture 15).

13   14   15

Whichever route you chose, you will emerge at a lane (picture 16). Turn right and continue along the lane, through the two bollards (picture 17) and up the hill until you reach a junction (picture 18).

16   17   18

Turn left at the junction and walk along the path through two hedges (picture 19) until you reach a kiss gate (picture 20). There is a yellow footpath marker on a post on the right-hand side. Go through the gate and turn immediately right, walk up across the field and along a track between two hedgerows (picture 21).

19   20   21

When you reach a fork, turn left and walk along the left-hand side of a hedge (pictures 22). The Dover Patrol Memorial can be seen in the distance. Carry on back to the start.

22

Stanstead

(3.5 miles)

This walk starts from Plaxdale Green Road, postcode TN15 7PB.

Find it on OS Explorer map 147: 62/59. The best way to get there (from Brands Hatch) is to take the last turning on the left after West Kingsdown and before the top of Wrotham Hill. When you turn into the road, after a few yards it splits left and right. Straight ahead of you is the Hill Top restaurant and hotel. Dating from the 1800s, this is a family run affair serving excellent meals on Friday and Saturday evenings and Sunday lunch. Diners can stay overnight in one of the bespoke bedrooms. We have dined here many times, whether in a group of four or a party of fourteen. The décor is superb with a roaring fire in the bar in the winter months. Tel: 01732 822696 Postcode TN15 7NY. Anyway, back to the walk…facing the Hill Top restaurant, take the left-hand road, which bears to the right after a short while and carry on down the road until you see a layby on the right just after Hollands farm and before Parsons Lane (main picture, looking back up the road). Park here and walk back up towards the cottage on the right (picture 1). Go through the kiss gate next to the cottage (picture 2) and walk straight across the field to the corner, to a stile with a lane and a cottage beyond (picture 3) Don't worry if you can't see the stile - have faith, because you will not see it until you are almost upon it.

| 1 | 2 | 3 |

Turn left and walk up the lane until you reach a bridleway on the right just past Harvest Cottage (picture 4). Walk along this bridle way at the edge of a field until you reach a fork (picture 5). Ignore the bridleway to the right (known as Wise's Lane) and walk straight ahead through the trees, until you reach a footpath sign on the right (picture 6). This sign shows two directions, ignore the right hand one that goes diagonally across the field, but take the path that goes straight across the field to the trees in picture 6.

4   5   6

At the corner of the trees, you will see a memorial stone to the South Ash Airfield (pictures 7 & 8). This area was used as an airfield by the RAF and the RFC during WW1, between 1916 and 1919. It was used for home defence squadrons before reverting to farm land. Carry on alongside the tree line and into Baker's wood. Halfway through the wood you will cross over a dilapidated stile (picture 9).

7   8   9

Continue over it until you reach a lane. Turn right and walk past the Stanstead water treatment works and you will come to a gate and a stile (picture 10). The path goes slightly upwards until you reach a kiss gate (picture 12). Carry on until you reach two kiss gates together (picture 12). Go through both gates, crossing fields with horses…

10 11 12

…and through to more kiss gates (pictures 13 & 14), where you will emerge onto Hatham Green Lane. Turn left and just past Hatham Green Cottage, you will see a narrow path on the right with a footpath sign (picture 15).

13 14 15

This short path leads to a lane with a bridleway opposite (picture 16). Walk along the bridleway until you see a marker post (picture 17) follow the red marker 209, through the wood with a challenging uphill climb, until you reach a gate (picture 18). Houses were in the process of being built when we did this walk, which should be completed by now!

16   17   18

Turn right and go through another gate into a field and head for a gap in the trees to the right (picture 19). Head down the track and through the gate where you will see another marker post (pictures 20 & 21).

19   20   21

Walk across the field to a stile (picture 22) and then across another field, heading for a stile between a house and a barn (pictures 23 & 24).

22   23   24

Go through the gate (picture 25), past the converted barn, back on to Plaxdale Green Road. Walk past the telephone box (picture 26) and carry on until you reach the start of the walk.

25   26

Tatsfield

(4.5 miles)

This walk starts from the Aperfield inn, 311, Main road Biggin Hill, TN16 2HN. If you park in the pub's car park, you must register the registration number inside; otherwise you will receive parking fine! We parked along the road. They serve a couple of real ales in this lovely well decorated inn (Doombar when we visited) and dogs are very welcome. There are a couple of steep inclines on this walk through the woodland, but generally it is flat. We did this walk in December when the temperature was -2⁰C.

With your back to the pub, turn left and carefully cross the road. After a few yards you will come to a footpath sign (picture 1). Take this narrow path (picture 2). Carry straight on, ignoring the gates to the left and right (picture 3).

1   2   3

You will eventually come to a cottage (picture 4). Walk down to the lane and turn right, walking past the cottage which is on your right (picture 5). After a short walk, you will see that the road splits. Turn left and follow the track (picture 6).

4   5   6

You will eventually come to a road sign and mail box (picture 7). Turn left and after a few paces, turn right along Parkwood Road (picture 8). You will pass some houses on both sides of the road until you come to a post on the left with a yellow arrow (picture 9). Turn left and walk along the narrow path between a fence and woodland.

7   8   9

At the end of the wood, climb over the stile and walk diagonally across the field (pictures 10 & 11), until you see a stile halfway along a fence (picture 12).

10   11   12

Walk across this field until you reach a stile next to a gate, with some farm buildings (picture 13). Walk past the buildings, up the lane with fields on either side until you reach a gate and a stile leading to a lane (picture 14). Turn right on the lane and after about five paces, turn left, over the defunct stile (picture 15) and continue along the path.

13   14   15

The path weaves left and right, with a high wooden fence on the right, until you reach the North Downs Way (picture 16). Turn left and walk along the North Downs way until you reach Westerham hill, with a footpath sign on the opposite of the road (picture 17). Carefully cross this fast and busy road and take the footpath alongside the field until you come to a kiss gate leading to a path through the woods (picture 18).

| 16 | 17 | 18 |

There are breath taking views across Kent as you walk along the top of the hill. When you reach the end of the field you will see a post and some steps on the left (picture 19). Go up the steps to another kiss gate (picture 20) and walk up the field, ignoring the path to the right, to another kiss gate (picture 21) and bear right through the woods.

| 19 | 20 | 21 |

Eventually you will come to some farm buildings and a cottage with a gate and stile between them (picture 22). Turn left on the lane and take the second stile on the right, after the house called "The Grays" (pictures 23 & 24),

22   23   24

Walk diagonally across the field (full of sheep when we walked), following the footpath. This path takes you through a kiss gate (picture 25) and two stiles (pictures 26 & 27) and between two horses' fields until you reach Buckhurst Road.

25   26   27

Cross the road to the other stile (picture 28) and continue along until you reach two stiles, one straight ahead and one to the left (picture 29). Ignore the one to the left and take the stile straight ahead to yet another stile (picture 30) and continue on the path between a fenced field and a hedge.

28   29   30

There are several stiles on this path, but just carry straight on until you see two stiles (picture 31). Take the stile straight ahead and walk on, between two houses, back to the main road opposite the start of the walk.

31

Thurnham

(3 miles)

This walk starts from the Black Horse Inn and is mainly cross country with the second half on a very steep hill. If you are parking in the pub car park, please get permission from the landlord first. We ate in the pub after the walk and had a delicious Sunday lunch. The pub has lots of old oak beams and nooks and crannies for dining or just drinking and was festooned in hops hanging from the ceilings. There are several real ale pumps on the bar. There is B&B accommodation available. The Postcode is ME14 3LD Tel: 01622 737185. Find it on OS Explorer map 148: 80/57.

Turn right out of the car park and walk to the crossroads and turn right, looking down the hill (picture 1). There are no paths on this lane and so keep an eye out for traffic. Walk down the lane, past the houses, until you come to a narrow path on the right that leads to St. Mary's church (picture 2). Walk through the graveyard, which has a yew tree reported to be over 1,000 years old, until you come to a gate that leads into a vineyard (picture 3).

1 2 3

Turn right (picture 4) and then bear left and walk between the vines (picture 5) until you reach a gap in the hedge (picture 6).

4 5 6

At the other end of the field, go through the gate (picture 7), and walk along the narrow path until you reach a road (picture 8). Turn right and walk up to the Cock Horse pub (picture 9) and turn right into the narrow lane opposite the pub. Be careful in this lane, as there are no paths.

7 8 9

Immediately after the cricket ground on the left, go through the gap in the hedge (picture 10) and walk up the hill. It bends to the right before reaching a gate with a sign that has an acorn arrow and the words "North Downs Way" (picture 11). Continue up and along the ridge with amazing views over the Kent countryside (picture 12).

10 11 12

Carry on along the well-trodden path, past the marker post (picture 13) and turn right and head down some very steep steps (picture 14) until you come to a kiss gate (picture 15).

13   14   15

Follow the path up to the two trees (picture 16). There are some more steps at the first tree. Walk along until you reach a gate and a kiss gate (picture 17) At this point you can turn right and walk back to the start, but if you turn left and walk up the hill for a few yards, you will see an entrance to the old Thurham castle, which was built in the 11th century and abandoned in the 15th century (picture 18). Then retrace your steps to the lane and head downhill back to the start and a refreshing drink (or two!).

16   17   18

Wateringbury

(5 miles)

This is a fairly flat walk with just a couple of gradual inclines. There is limited parking in Love Lane (ME18 5NZ), which is opposite the start of the walk. If you do park in Love Lane, carefully walk back across the busy road and take the track between the houses (picture 1) and up past the red litter bin (picture 2) to a gate with a path to the right (picture 3) this path to the right is where you will emerge at the end of the walk, so take the path ahead beside the gate and through the wood.

1   2   3

Carry on along the path (picture 4). You should come to a large felled tree (picture 5) and then a fork in the path with a marker post (picture 6).

4   5   6

Take the left-hand fork. This path follows the PLUTO pipeline (picture 7). It stands for Pipeline Under The Ocean and is one of three pipelines that supplied troops with fuel during world war II. There are pumping station on the coast at Greatstone and Shanklin on the Isle of Wight, which were disguised as ordinary houses to fool the German reconnaissance planes. The troops working in the areas wore civilian clothes to further fool the Germans. Carry on, ignoring the track to the right, past the coppiced wood of sweet chestnut on the left (picture 8). When the track bends to the left, look carefully to the right – there is a not very well defined path (picture 9)…

7   8   9

…that leads to a lane called Teston Road (picture 10). Turn left and walk down the road for a short while (picture 11), until you see a footpath sign pointing right (picture 12).

10   11   12

This path leads through Kings Hill Sports park (picture 13). Carry on until you reach a track through the woods (picture 14) and take the right fork (picture 15).

13   14   15

Walk alongside the woodland (picture 16), ignoring the track to the right (picture 17), until you reach another forked track (picture 18). Take the right-hand fork.

16   17   18

The path leads to the right of a fence (picture 19) and eventually to a lane called "The Heath" (picture 20). Turn right and walk along the lane (picture 21)…

19   20   21

…until you reach a crossroads (picture 22). Carefully cross this road to sweeps lane and on the right, you will see a path through the woodlands (picture 23). Keep walking straight ahead (picture 24), ignoring all cross tracks.

22   23   24

The path narrows at a marker post (picture 25) and eventually to North Pole Road (picture 26). Turn left and almost immediately there is a byway on the right (picture 27).

25   26   27

Carry on along this byway until you reach some houses. Just before a pond on the right, opposite a house, there is a path with a post with a blue arrow marker (picture 28). Take this path until you reach footpath sign and marker post showing a path to the left (picture 29). When you reach a lane (picture 30), turn right…

28   29   30

…and walk towards some houses until you see a footpath sign on the left (picture 31). Take this path up to another road and cross to the other side and take the path (pictures 32 & 33).

31   32   33

This will lead you to another road. Turn left and walk a short way to a lane with footpath sign on the other side of the road (picture 34). This will take you to Red Hill farm, where the footpath signs disappear, but carry on past the house and then turn left to walk down between the house and outbuildings (picture 35). Continue along the track (picture 36)…

34   35   36

…until it turns to the right by a gate (picture 37). Follow the track (picture 38), past poly tunnels on your left, until you reach path where you were at picture 3. Turn left and walk back down to the start of the walk (picture 39).

37   38   39

West Kingsdown No.1

(1 ½ miles)

This is a very short walk around the pretty Church woods. The church of St. Edmund King & Martyr is said to date back to around 1030AD and is definitely worth a visit. A small free information booklet is available inside the church, which tells that St. Edmund was a Christian king of East Anglia until around 870AD, when he was captured and killed by the invading Danes. He was later buried at Bury St. Edmunds – where else! The woods are just behind Brands hatch racing circuit on Fawkham Road. The church does not have a postcode, but the postcode for the cottages opposite the end of the lane is TN15 6AX.

Park in the church carpark, and the walk starts at the lychgate (see picture 1). Walk around the left-hand side of the church past the yew tree reported to be 1,000 years old, to a path into the woods (picture 2). After a few yards, take the right fork (picture 3).

1   2   3

This will lead you to Fawkham road (picture 4). Turn left and walk towards the cottages on the left (Picture 5), until you come to a footpath sign (picture 6). Turn left along the footpath.

4   5   6

Carry on straight ahead between fields of horses (picture 7) and at the end, turn left (picture 8) and walk along the narrow path back to the woodlands (picture 9).

7   8   9

Carry on along the path, keeping the houses on your right until you reach a cycle barrier (picture 10). Turn immediately left and through another barrier (picture 11). When the path comes to a wide track (picture 12), turn right.

10   11   12

The wide track soon narrows, but continue to follow the winding path all the way back to the lane to the carpark (picture 13). Turn left and walk back to the start.

13

West Kingsdown No.2

(4.5 miles)

This is a very challenging walk over steep hills, with a heart thumping climb near the end! This walk is not for those with a weak disposition. As parking along the A20 is difficult, it may be advisable to park in a street nearby to Blewers timber merchants. Postcode TN15 6BT. On a Sunday, it is possible to park outside Blewers, between the gates.

The walk starts at a footpath that leads between the timber merchants and other commercial properties (see picture 1). Follow this path until you emerge onto a field (picture 2). Cross the field to a kiss gate (picture 3) and onto a quiet road.

| 1 | 2 | 3 |

After a short walk along this road, the path turns left through a field with large pile of flint stones (picture 4). Continue until you come to a kiss gate and an opening (picture 5). Walk diagonally right down this field to a stile in the hedge (picture 6).

4   5   6

This leads to another field and another stile (picture 7) and again to a kiss gate at the corner of the house (picture 8). The path here is not very well marked, but keeps going diagonally; down to a stile that leads you on to Maplescombe lane (picture 9).

7   8   9

Turn left along this quiet road and walk past all the houses until you reach a footpath sign on the right, at the junction of Maplescombe Lane, Knatts Valley Road and Botsom lane (picture 10) This path and track had been churned up and muddy when I returned in January. Turn right and walk up this track. Just before you reach a gate, the path turns left (picture 11). Continue along this path with great views to the left, through a small wooded area, until it meets houses (picture 12).

10   11   12

Turn left and continue along the road, past the holiday homes and farm house to a footpath on the left (picture 13). This leads to some very steep steps down with a hand rail (picture 14) When you reach Knatts Valley road, turn left and after you pass a large brick building on the right, there is a byway and then a footpath up through a field (picture 15) which leads to a steep path with steps. You may need to get your breath back halfway up!

13   14 – looking back up   15

At the top (picture 16), turn left and follow the byway, ignoring the footpath on the right (picture 17), until you reach a quiet road with houses on both sides (picture 18). Follow this road as it bends to the right and eventually you will emerge onto the A20, through the middle of West Kingsdown. Turn left and walk about ½ mile back to the beginning.

16   17   18

Wrotham

(4 miles)

This walk starts a Labour in vain road, Wrotham (pronounced, "Routeham"). Park safely along the road near the Hilltop Hotel & Restaurant, Postcode TN15 7NY. The walk has some steep climbs and some very rough fields and byways, so I recommend that you wear stout footwear.

To the right of the hotel, you will see a gate and a stile (picture 1) Cross into the field and walk alongside the rear of the hotel (picture 2) until you reach a gate that leads into a mobile home park (picture 3).

1   2   3

Turn right and walk along the road and into the woods (picture 4) Follow the path through the woods until you reach a stile leading into a field (picture 5). Walk diagonally right up the field until you reach a stile (picture 6).

4 5 6

Don't cross the stile, but turn right and follow the edge of the field (picture 7). When you reach a gate, with your back to the gate, follow the footpath across the field towards the tree line (picture 8) and eventually you will reach a gate (picture 9).

7 8 9

The path is not defined here and be aware that this ploughed field is very bumpy so watch your ankles! Walk diagonally left up the field until you see a stile on the opposite side of the field, leading to Labour in Vain lane (picture 10). Cross the lane, go through the kiss gate and walk diagonally left to a gate to a field with horses (picture 11) and then again walk diagonally left to a kiss gate (picture 12).

10   11   12

Eventually you will reach a gate with a dilapidated stile (pictures 13 & 14). Go across the field to another stile (picture 14).

13   14   15

You will now be on a bridle way (picture 16) Turn right and follow this bridle way past houses (picture 17) down a very steep and very rough path, until you reach a junction in the path, just before the Wrotham hill road. Take the path to the right, which leads to the road. Turn left and walk down the road until you see the footpath sign and bridge on the other side of the road (picture 18) Very carefully cross this very busy and fast road and then cross the bridge over the M20.

16   17   18

At the other side, when you reach the road, turn left (picture 19) and walk down until you see a byeway on the right (picture 20). Follow this byeway straight ahead, ignoring the road to the left (picture 21).

19	20	21

This is the North Downs Way (picture 22). Keep going straight ahead and eventually you will reach a road (picture 23). Turn right and walk up the road. Just before the road bears left, there is a narrow path on your right (picture 24). Take this path up through the woods...

22	23	24

...until you reach a footbridge over a road (picture 25) Follow the path across the fields and through the gates (pictures 26 & 27).

25   26   27

You will emerge onto the West Kingsdown road (picture 28). Carefully cross the road, through the gap opposite, back to the start.

28

Printed in Great Britain
by Amazon

46851514R00090